This book belongs to
Este libro pertenece a

Illustrations by Paula Knight (Advocate)
English language consultant: Betty Root

This edition published by Parragon Books Ltd in 2015
and distributed by:

Parragon Inc.
440 Park Avenue South,
13th Floor
New York, NY 10016, USA
www.parragon.com

ISBN 978-1-4748-1505-5

Printed in China

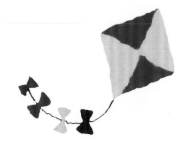

My First
100
WORDS

• • • • • •

Mis primeras
100
PALABRAS

SPANISH and ENGLISH . ESPAÑOL e INGLÉS

PaRragon

Bath • New York • Cologne • Melbourne • Delhi
Hong Kong • Shenzhen • Singapore • Amsterdam

Mi familia
My family

Mamá
Mom

Papá
Dad

el hermano
brother

la hermana
sister

el bebé
baby

la abuela
grandma

el abuelo
grandpa

el perro
dog

En mi casa
In my home

la puerta
door

la ventana
window

la alfombra
rug

la televisión
television

la silla
chair

el sofá
sofa

la mesa
table

las flores
flowers

Mi ropa
Getting dressed

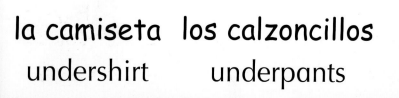

la camiseta
undershirt

los calzoncillos
underpants

el pantalón corto
shorts

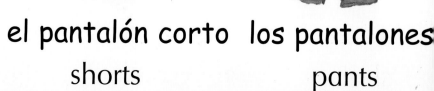

los pantalones
pants

la falda   **los calcetines**   **los zapatos**   **la camisa**   **el suéter**

skirt   socks   shoes   shirt   sweater

La comida
Mealtime

el tazón
bowl

el plato
plate

el jarro
pitcher

el cuchillo
knife

el tenedor
fork

la cuchara
spoon

la taza
cup

el platillo
saucer

La hora de jugar
Playtime

el tren
train

la trompeta
trumpet

el tambor
drum

los bloques de madera
blocks

la caja sorpresa
jack-in-the-box

la muñeca
doll

las pinturas
paints

el rompecabezas
puzzle

En la ciudad
In the city

el autobús
bus

el camión
truck

la tienda
store

la bicicleta
bicycle

el carro
car

el cochecito
stroller

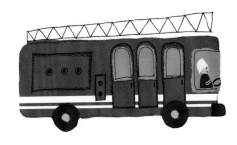

el coche de bomberos
fire truck

la moto
motorcycle

En el parque
In the park

los columpios
swings

el tobogán
slide

el subibaja
seesaw

la pelota
ball

la verja
gate

el árbol
tree

el pájaro
bird

la cometa
kite

Junto al mar
At the seashore

el cubo
pail

la pala
shovel

el helado
ice cream

el pez
fish

el castillo de arena
sandcastle

la playera
T-shirt

el cangrejo
crab

el barco
boat

la concha
shell

En la tienda
At the store

la canasta
basket

el carrito
cart

los plátanos
bananas

las manzanas
apples

las naranja
oranges

las zanahorias
carrots

el pan
bread

los tomates
tomatoes

la leche
milk

el queso
cheese

En la granja
On the farm

el caballo

horse

la vaca

cow

el granjero

farmer

el puerco

pig

la gallina
chicken

el gato
cat

la oveja
sheep

el tractor
tractor

La hora del baño
Bathtime

el cepillo para los dientes
toothbrush

la pasta de dientes
toothpaste

el baño
bathtub

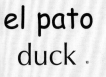 **el pato**
duck

el jabón
soap

la toalla
towel

 **el orinal de niño**
potty

la vasija
sink

A la cama
Bedtime

la lámpara

lamp

las pantuflas

slippers

la cama

bed

el reloj

clock

el libro
book

la luna
moon

el pijama
pajamas

el oso
teddy bear

Frases útiles   Useful phrases

| Hola | Hello |
| Adiós | Goodbye |

Sí	Yes
No	No
Por favor	Please
Gracias	Thank you

Buenos días	Good morning
Buenas tardes	Good afternoon
Buenas noches	Goodnight

| ¿Cómo te llamas? | What is your name? |
| Me llamo … | My name is … |

| ¿Cómo estás? | How are you? |
| Muy bien. | I am very well. |

| ¿Dónde vives? | Where do you live? |
| Vivo en … | I live in … |

¿Cuántos años tienes?
How old are you?

Tengo … años.
I am … years old.

Las partes del cuerpo Parts of the body

el pelo
hair

el ojo
eye

la oreja
ear

la nariz
nose

la boca
mouth

el cuello
neck

el brazo
arm

el pulgar
thumb

la mano
hand

el dedo
(de la mano)
finger

la pierna
leg

la rodilla
knee

el dedo (del pie)
toe

el pie
foot

Los días de la semana
Days of the week

lunes	Monday
martes	Tuesday
miércoles	Wednesday
jueves	Thursday
viernes	Friday
sábado	Saturday
domingo	Sunday

Los meses del año
Months of the year

enero	January
febrero	February
marzo	March
abril	April
mayo	May
junio	June
julio	July
agosto	August
septiembre	September
octubre	October
noviembre	November
diciembre	December

Los colores Colors

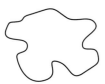 **blanco** white

 rojo red

 negro black

 **café** brown

 anaranjado orange

 rosa pink

 amarillo yellow

 **morado** purple

 **verde** green

azul blue

Los números Numbers

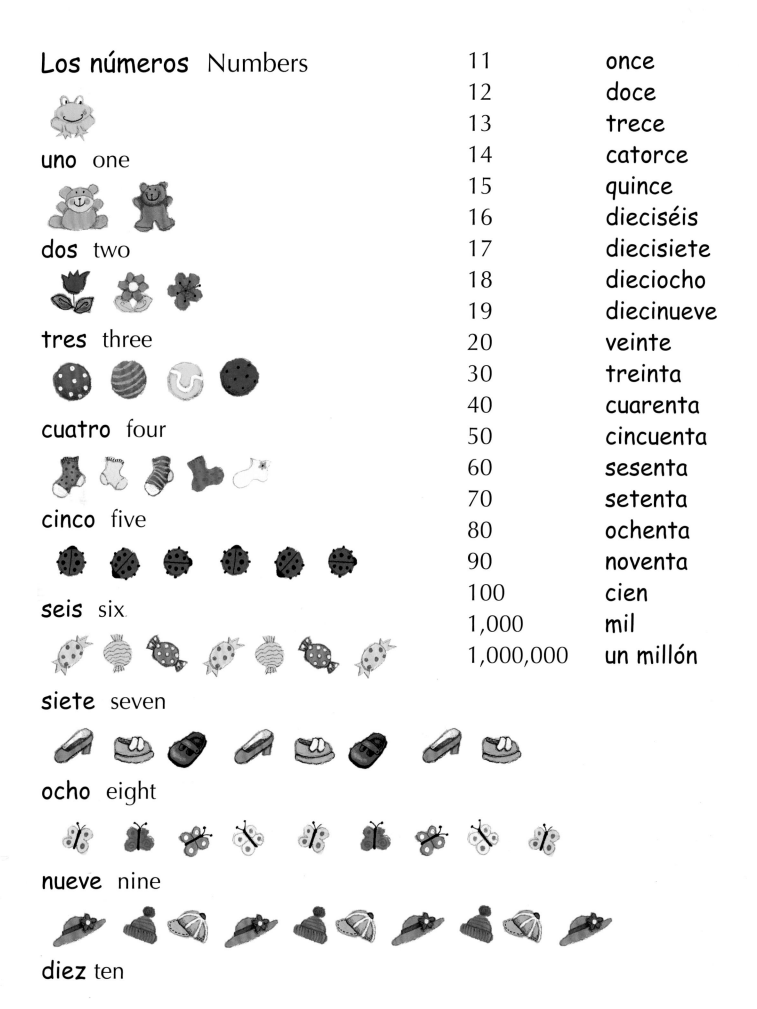

uno one

dos two

tres three

cuatro four

cinco five

seis six

siete seven

ocho eight

nueve nine

diez ten

11	once
12	doce
13	trece
14	catorce
15	quince
16	dieciséis
17	diecisiete
18	dieciocho
19	diecinueve
20	veinte
30	treinta
40	cuarenta
50	cincuenta
60	sesenta
70	setenta
80	ochenta
90	noventa
100	cien
1,000	mil
1,000,000	un millón

Word list

a

la abuela	*grandma*
el abuelo	*grandpa*
la alfombra	*rug*
amarillo	*yellow*
el árbol	*tree*
el autobús	*bus*
azul	*blue*

b

el baño	*bathtub*
el barco	*boat*
el bebé	*baby*
la bicicleta	*bicycle*
blanco	*white*
el bloque de madera	*block*
la boca	*mouth*
el brazo	*arm*

c

el caballo	*horse*
café	*brown*
la caja sorpresa	*jack-in-the-box*
el calcetín	*sock*
los calzoncillos	*underpants*
la cama	*bed*
el camión	*truck*
la camisa	*shirt*
la camiseta	*undershirt*
la canasta	*basket*
el cangrejo	*crab*
el carrito	*cart*
el carro	*car*
la casa	*house*
el castillo de arena	*sandcastle*
el cepillo para los dientes	*toothbrush*
la ciudad	*city*
el coche de bomberos	*fire truck*
el cochecito	*stroller*
los columpios	*swings*
la cometa	*kite*
la comida	*meal*
la concha	*shell*
el cubo	*pail*
la cuchara	*spoon*
el cuchillo	*knife*
el cuello	*neck*

d

el dedo (de la mano)	*finger*
el dedo (del pie)	*toe*

f

la falda	*skirt*
la familia	*family*
la flor	*flower*

g/h

la gallina	*hen*
el gato	*cat*
la granja	*farm*
el granjero	*farmer*
el helado	*ice cream*
la hermana	*sister*
el hermano	*brother*

j

el jabón	*soap*
el jarro	*pitcher*

l

la lámpara	*lamp*
la leche	*milk*
el libro	*book*
la luna	*moon*

m

Mamá	*Mom*
la mano	*hand*
la manzana	*apple*
el mar	*sea*
la mesa	*table*
morado	*purple*
la moto	*motorcycle*
la muñeca	*doll*

n/o

la naranja	*orange*
la nariz	*nose*
negro	*black*
el ojo	*eye*
la oreja	*ear*
el orinal de niño	*potty*
el oso	*teddy bear*
la oveja	*sheep*

p/q

el pájaro	*bird*
la pala	*shovel*
el pan	*bread*
el pantalón corto	*shorts*
los pantalones	*pants*
las pantuflas	*slippers*
Papá	*Dad*
el parque	*park*
la pasta de dientes	*toothpaste*
el pato	*duck*
la pelota	*ball*

el pelo	*hair*
el perro	*dog*
el pez	*fish*
el pie	*foot*
la pierna	*leg*
el pijama	*pajamas*
las pinturas	*paints*
el plátano	*banana*
el platillo	*saucer*
el plato	*plate*
la playera	*T-shirt*
el puerco	*pig*
la puerta	*door*
el pulgar	*thumb*
el queso	*cheese*

r

el reloj	*clock*
la rodilla	*knee*
rojo	*red*
el rompecabezas	*puzzle*
la ropa	*clothes*
rosa	*pink*

s

la silla	*chair*
el sofá	*sofa*
el subibaja	*seesaw*
el suéter	*sweater*

t

la taza	*cup*
el tazón	*bowl*
la televisión	*television*
el tambor	*drum*
el tenedor	*fork*
la tienda	*store*
la toalla	*towel*
el tobogán	*slide*
el tomate	*tomato*
el tractor	*tractor*
el tren	*train*
la trompeta	*trumpet*

v

la vaca	*cow*
la vasija	*sink*
la ventana	*window*
verde	*green*
la verja	*gate*

z

la zanahoria	*carrot*
el zapato	*shoe*